Coloring book for adults and kids vehicles image for design

This coloring book is belongs to

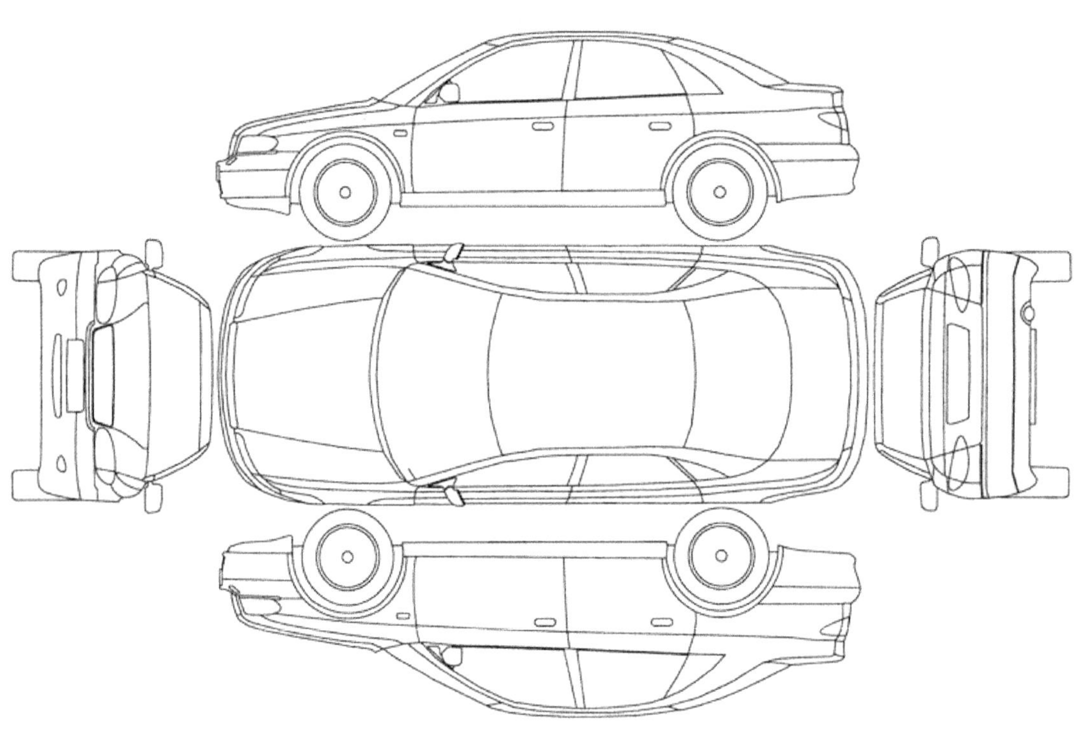

SAR NH869
COASTGUARD
POLICE
0369
AMBULANCE
96
369
369

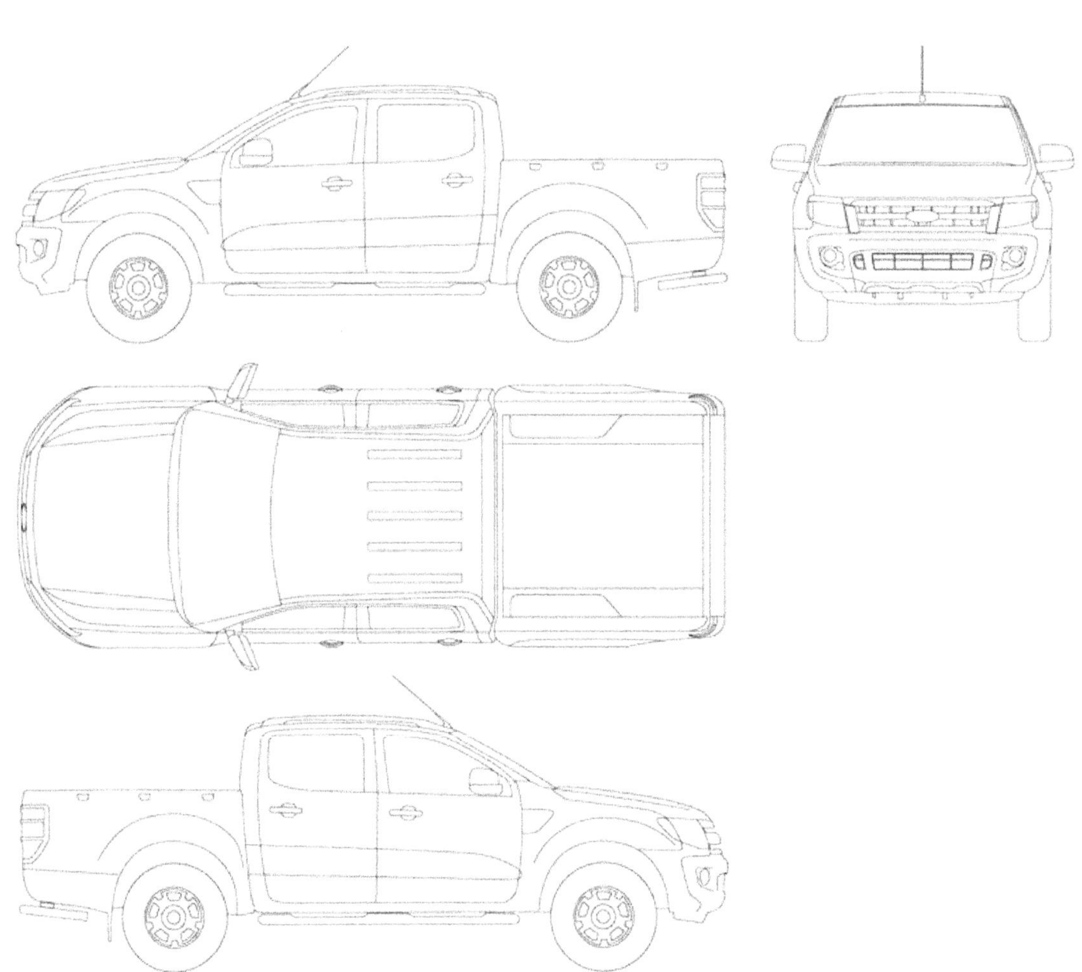

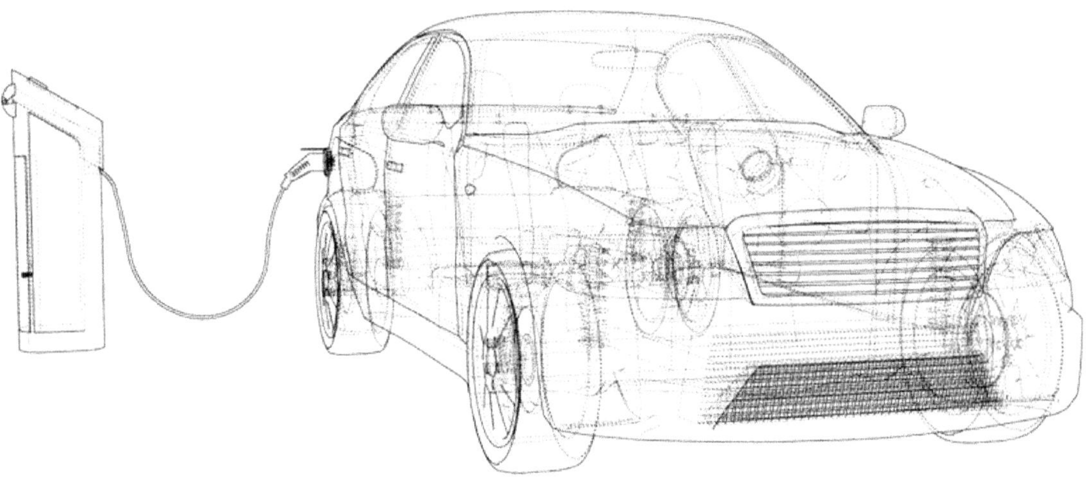

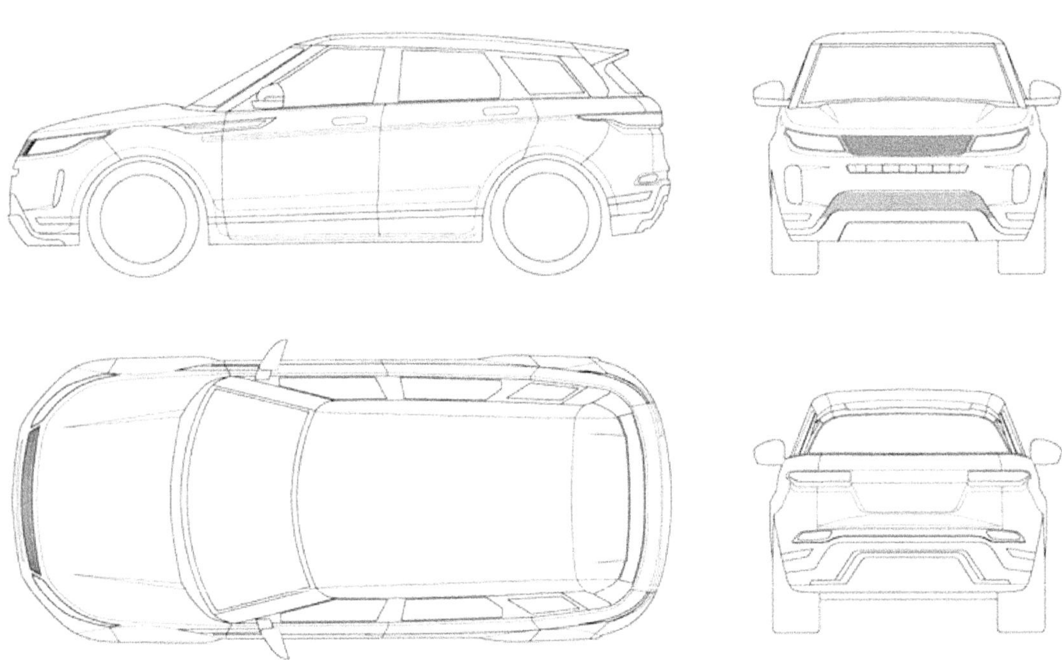

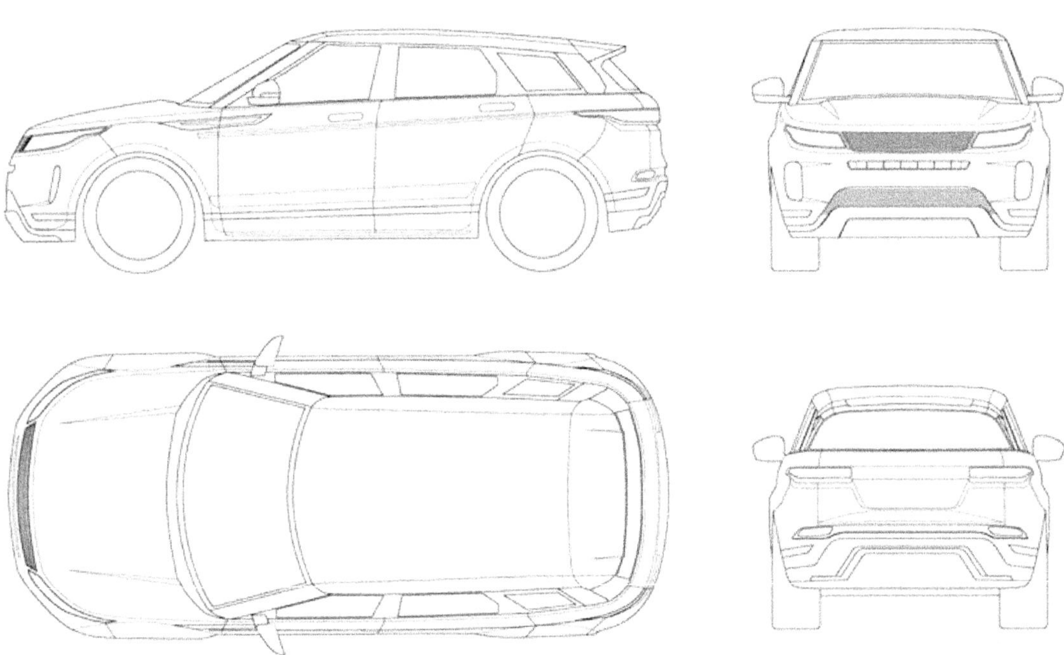

Vehicles

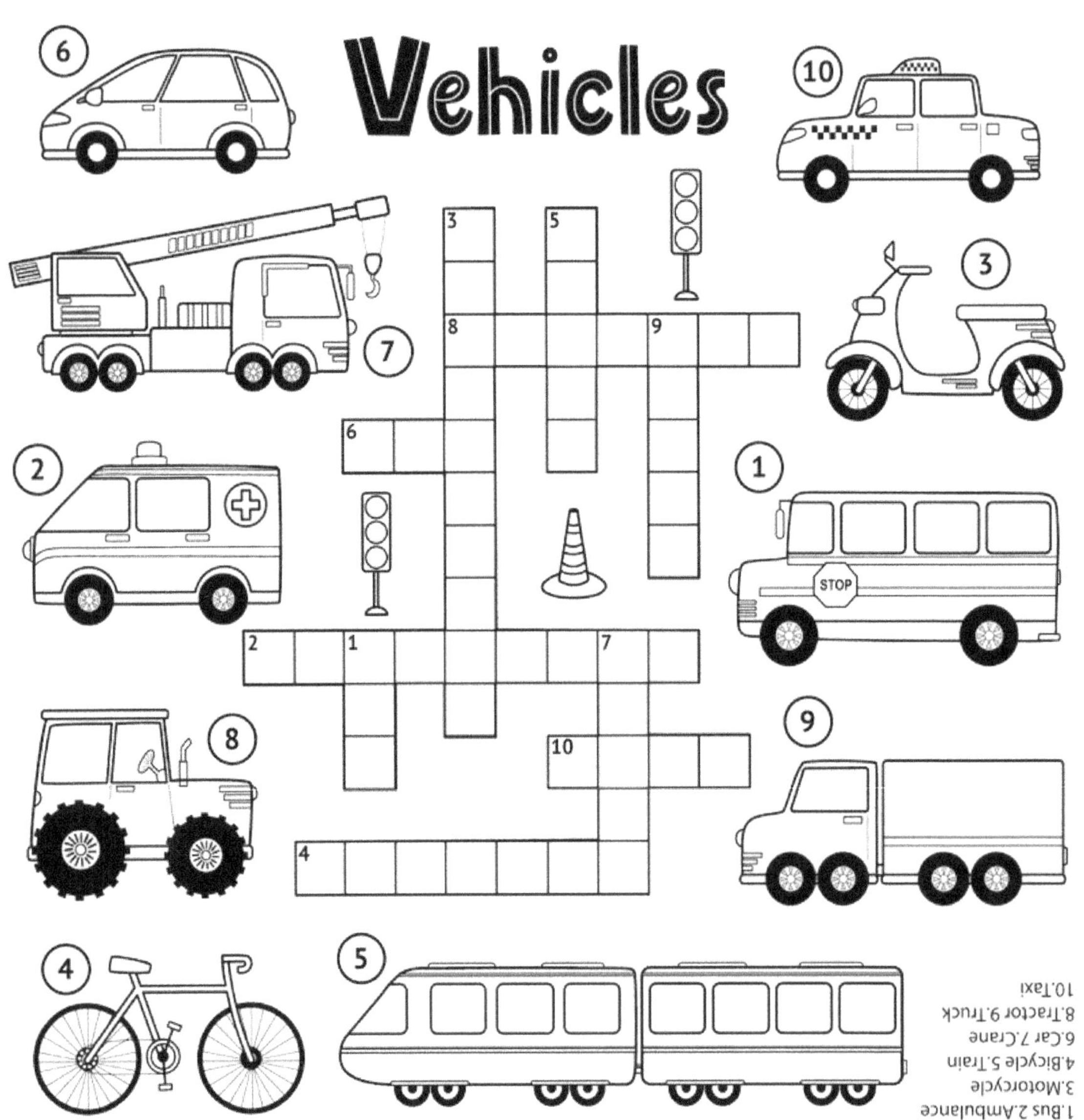

1.Bus 2.Ambulance
3.Motorcycle
4.Bicycle 5.Train
6.Car 7.Crane
8.Tractor 9.Truck
10.Taxi

Trafic
City
TAXI

OFFROAD

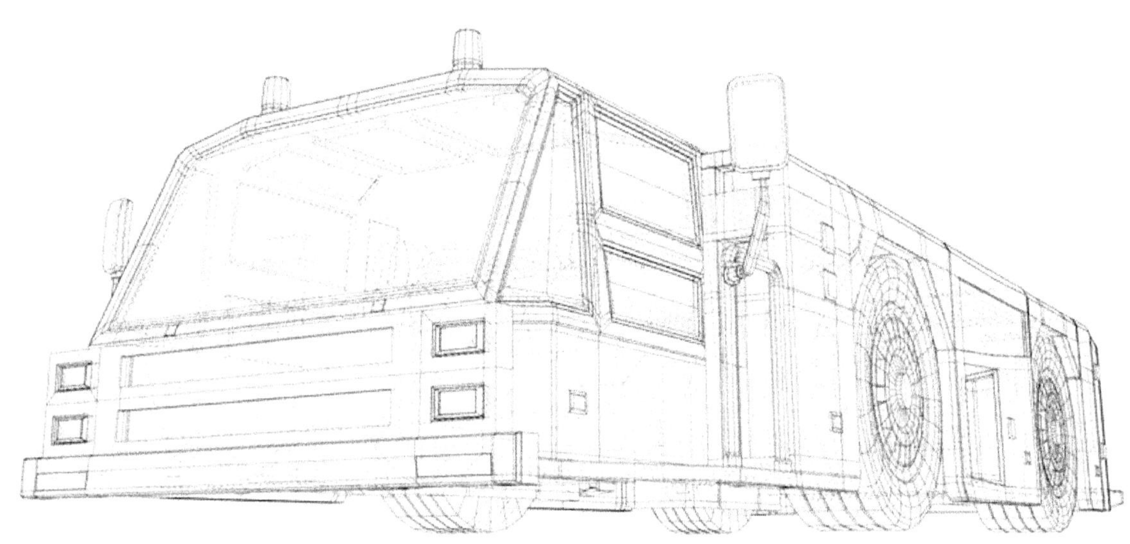

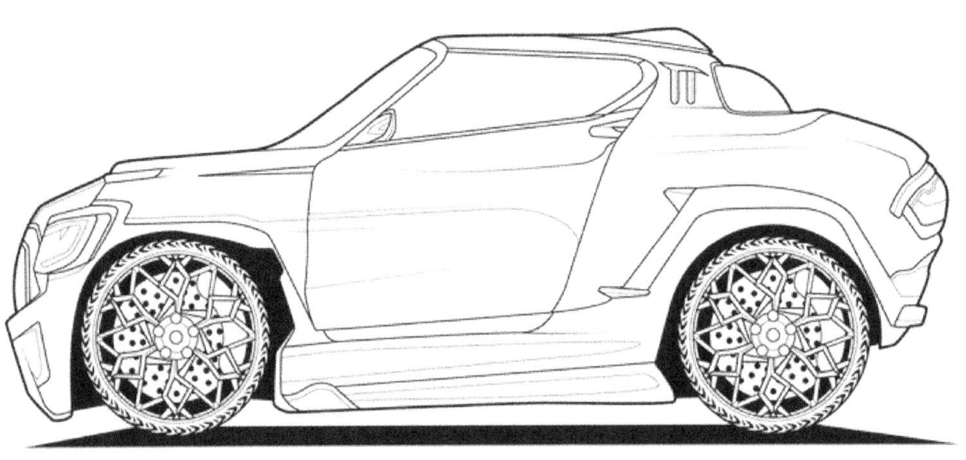

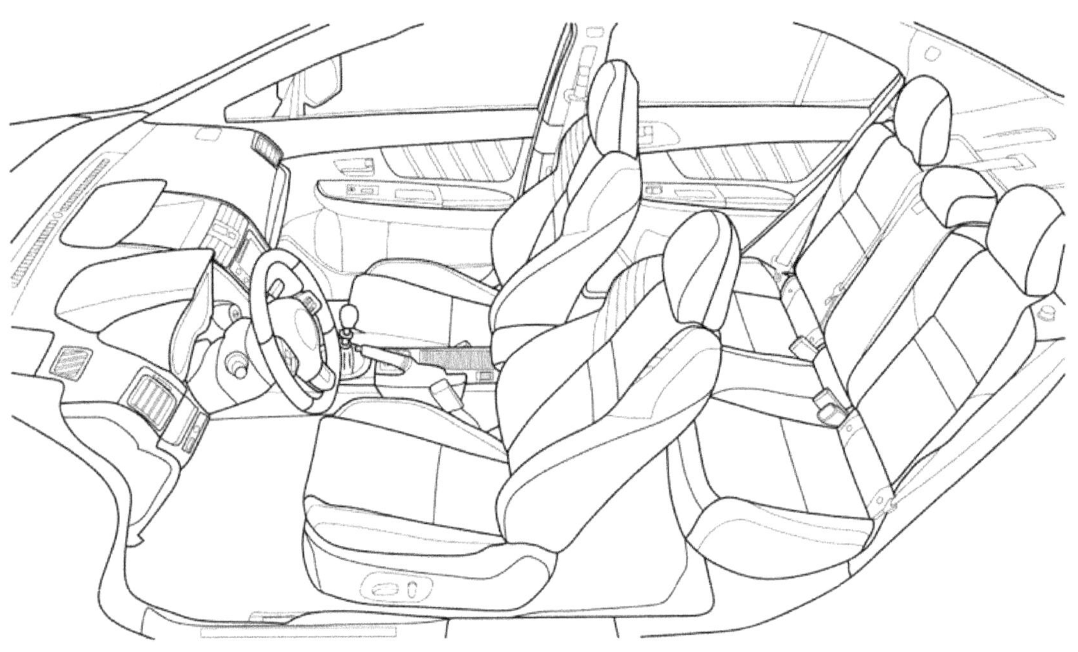

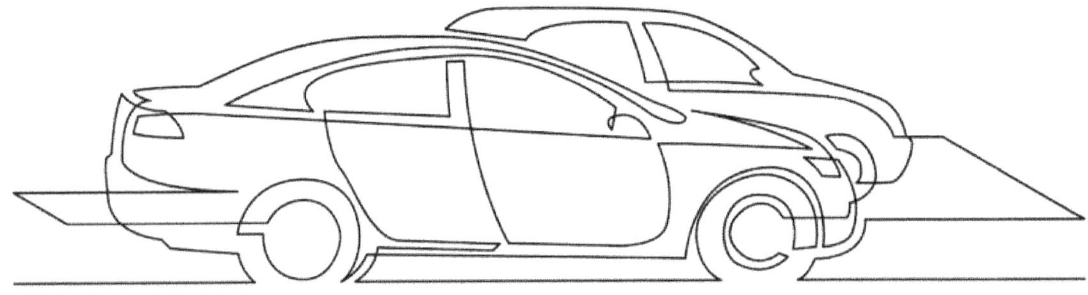

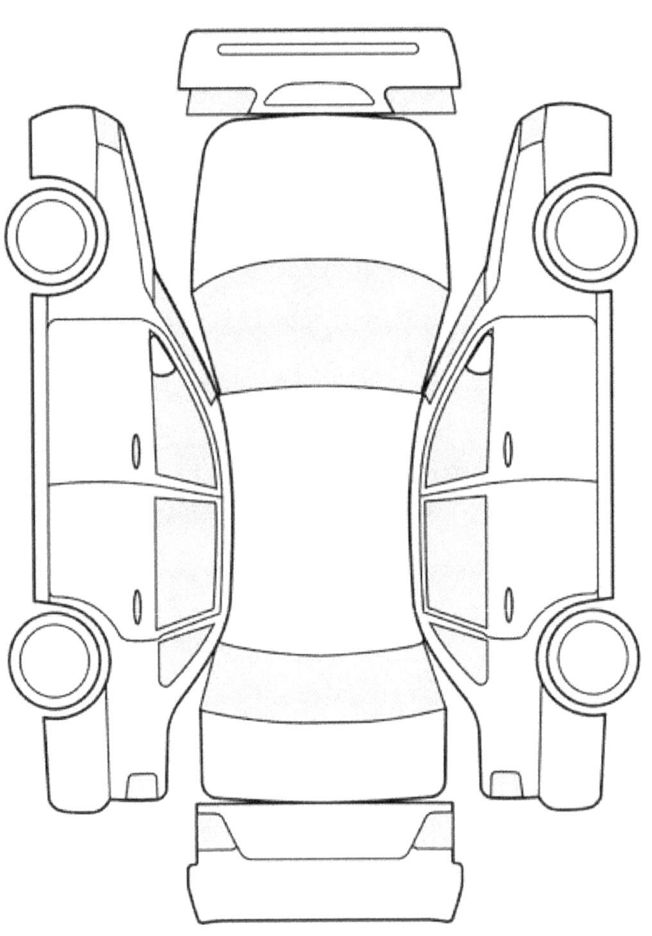